Tenor Sax Sheet Music With Lettered Noteheads Book 1

20 Easy Pieces For Beginners

Michael Shaw

Copyright © 2017 Michael Shaw. All rights reserved. Including the right to reproduce this book or portions thereof, in any form. No part of this text may be reproduced in any form without the express written permission of the author.

Music Arrangements. All arrangements in this book by
Michael Shaw Copyright © 2017

ISBN: 1544837682
ISBN-13: 978-1544837680

www.mikesmusicroom.co.uk

Contents

After The Ball	1
Amazing Grace	4
Beautiful Dreamer	6
Camptown Races	8
Caprice	12
Daisy Bell	18
Fur Elise	21
Eine Kleine Nachtmusik	24
Home On The Range	28
Liebestraum	32
Lullabye	36
Michael Row the Boat Ashore	38
My Heart At Thy Sweet Voice	40
Oh Susanna	43
Piano Concerto No 1	46
When The Saints Go Marching In	48
Sonata Pathetique	52
Valse Lente	54
The Yellow Rose Of Texas	58
Trumpet Voluntary	62
About The Author	66

After The Ball

Charles K. Harris

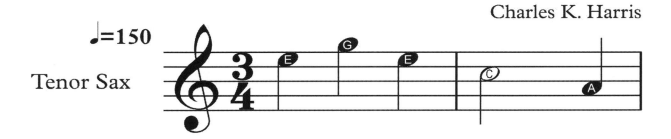

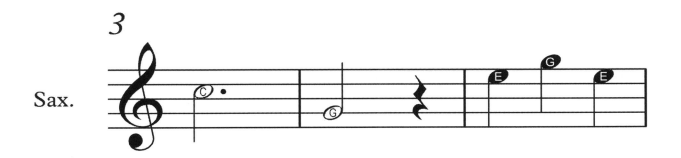

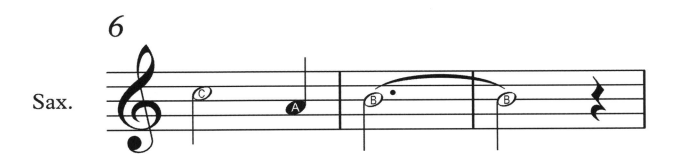

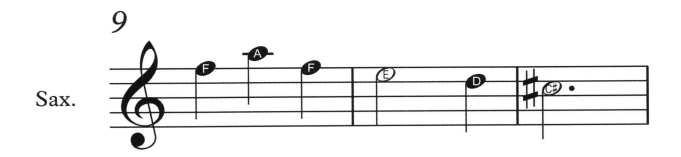

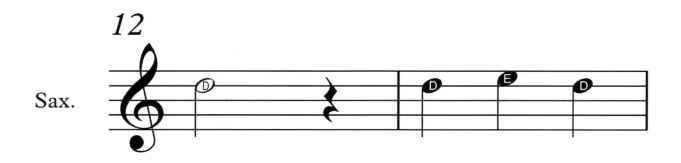
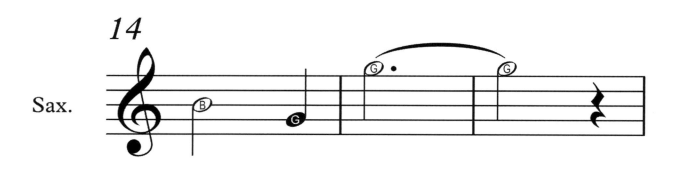
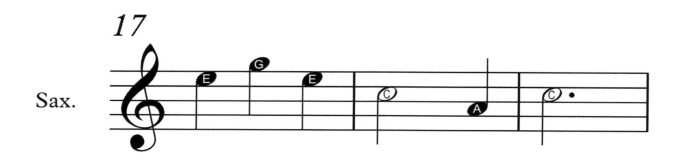
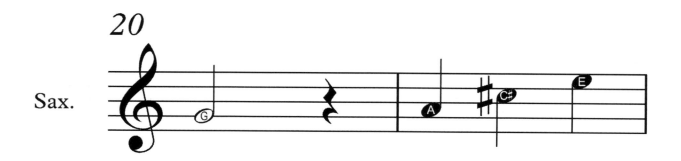

2

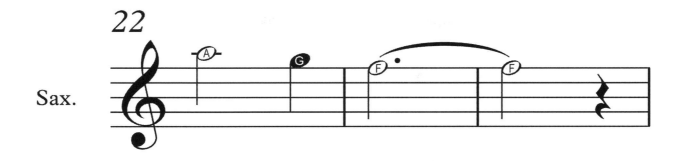
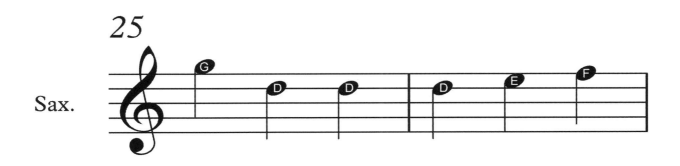
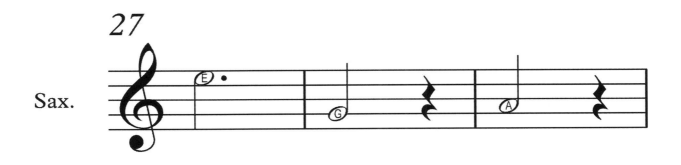
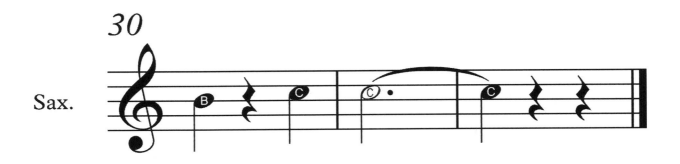

Amazing Grace

John Newton

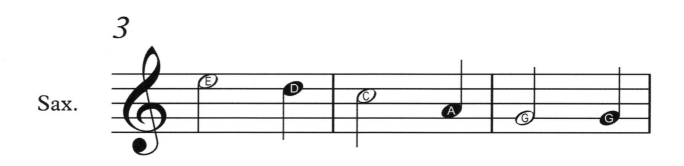

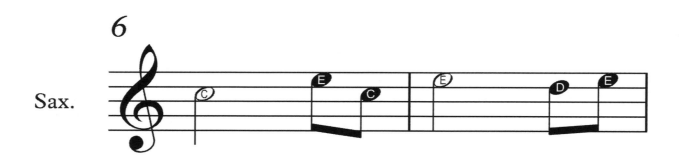

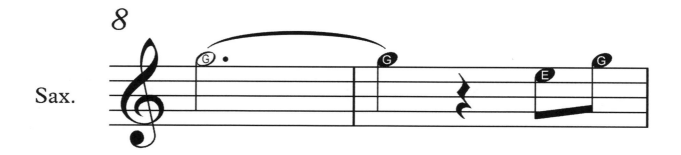

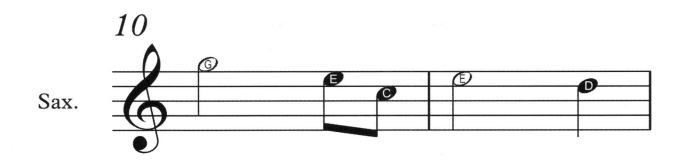

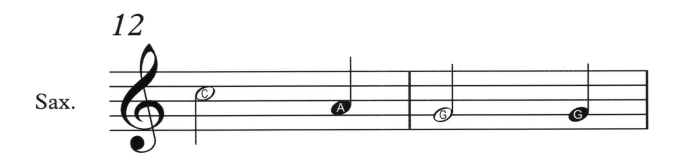

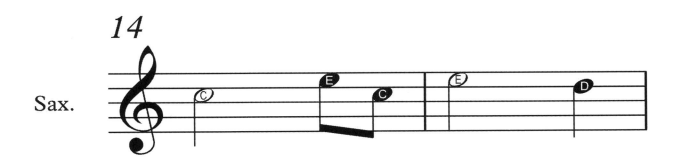

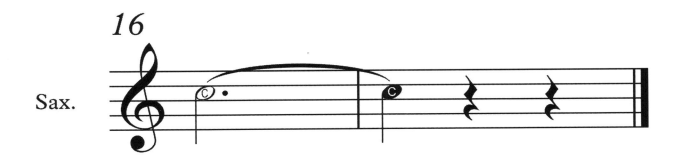

Beautiful Dreamer

Stephen Collins Foster

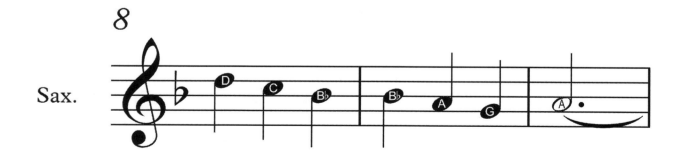

Camptown Races

Stephen Collins Foster

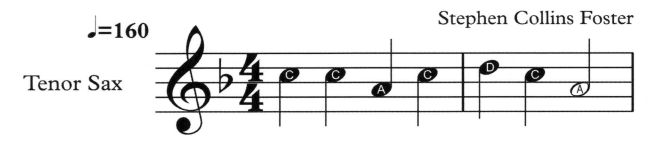
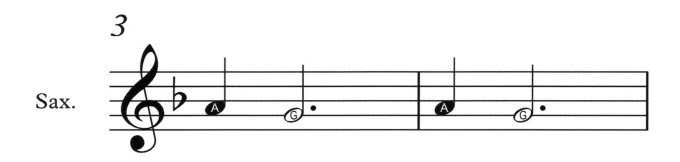
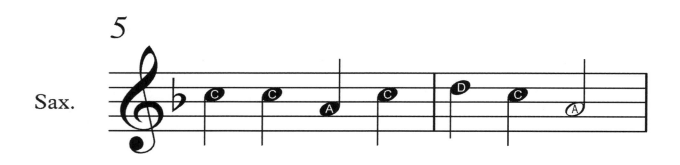
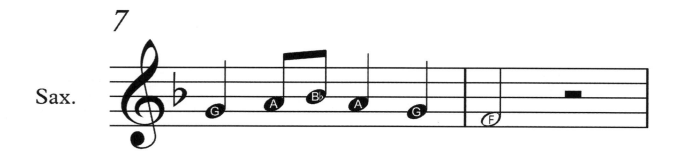

8

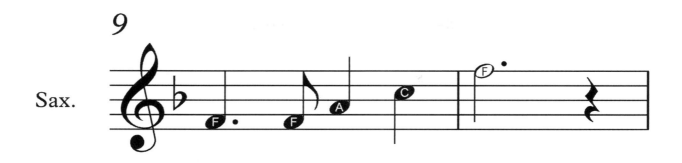
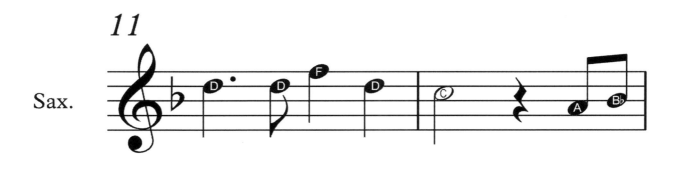
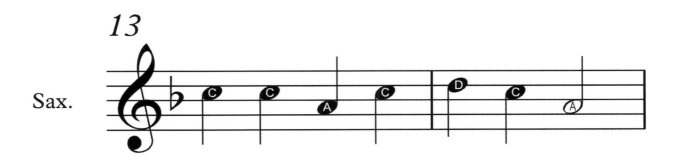
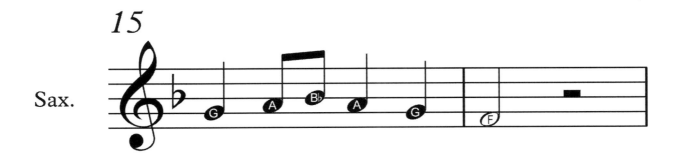

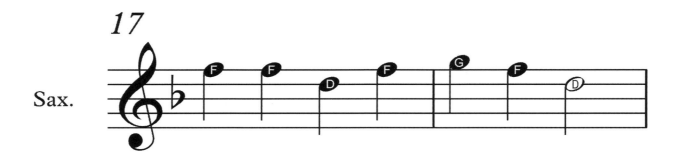

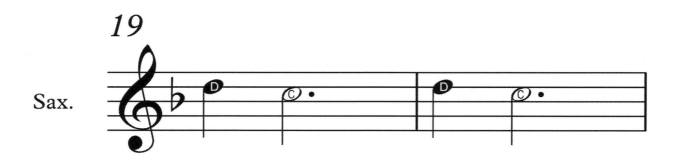

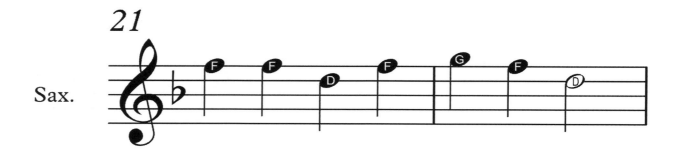

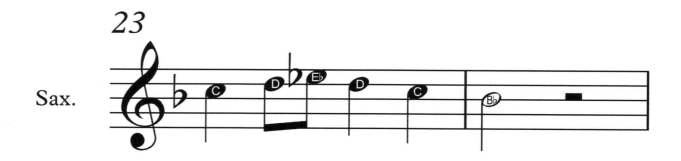

25

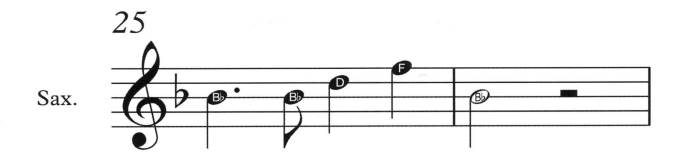

27

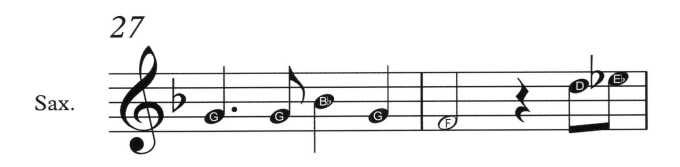

29

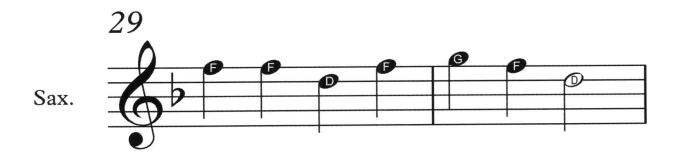

31

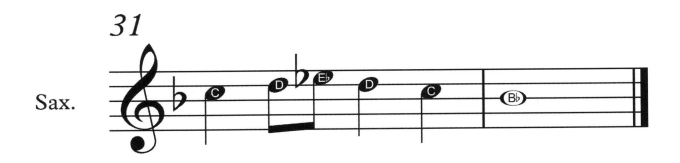

Caprice

Paganini

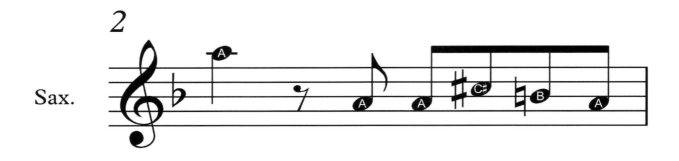

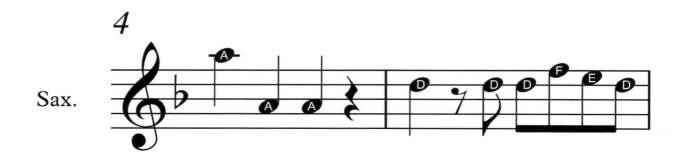

Daisy Bell

Henry Dacre

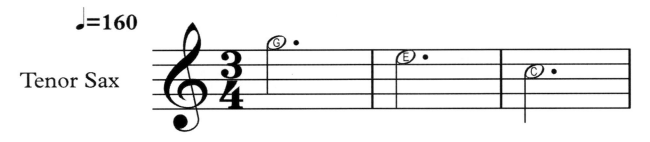

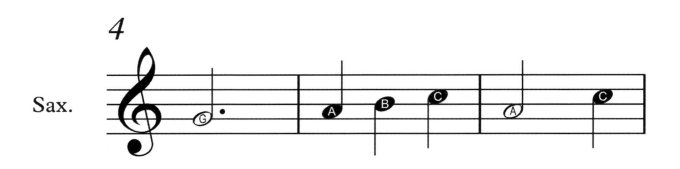

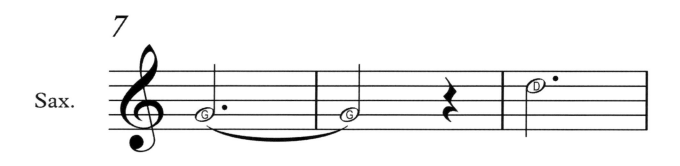

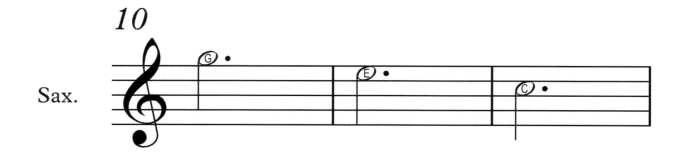

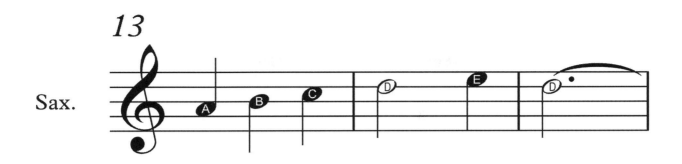
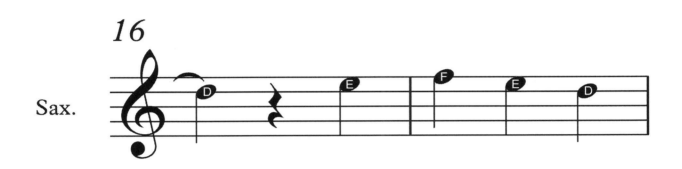
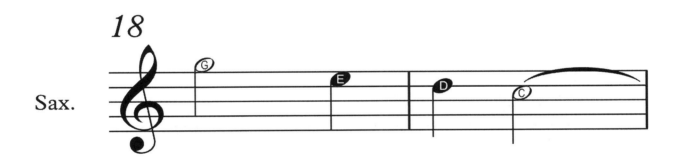
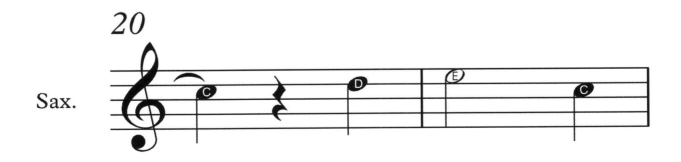

Fur Elise

Beethoven

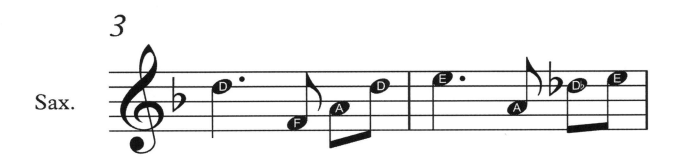

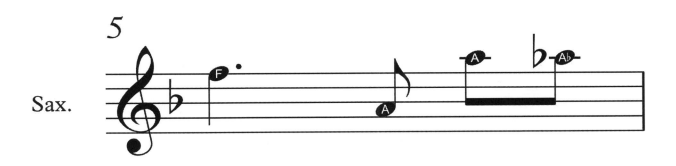

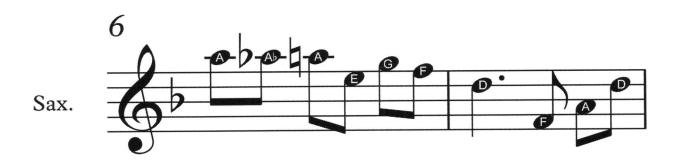

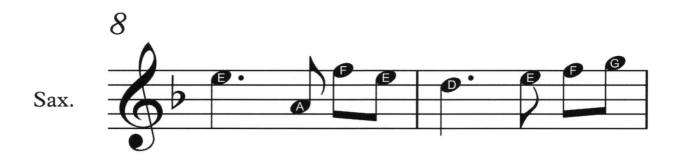
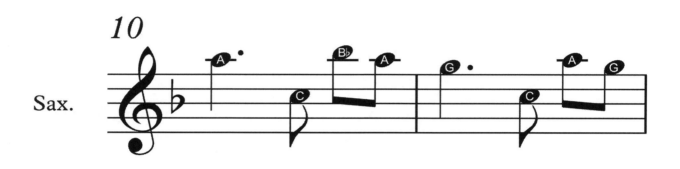
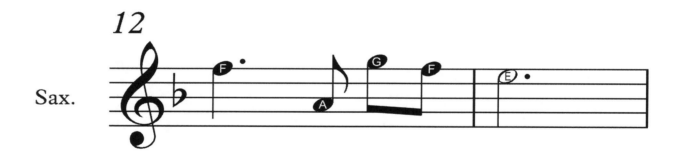
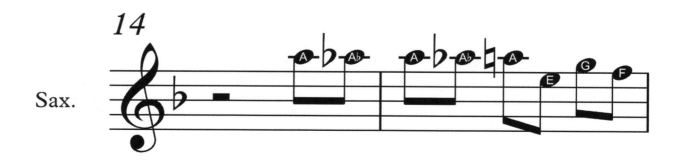

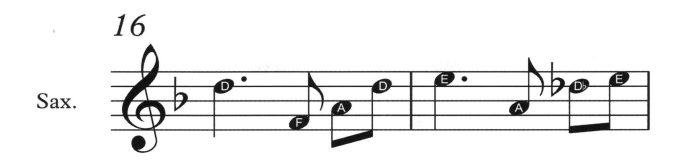
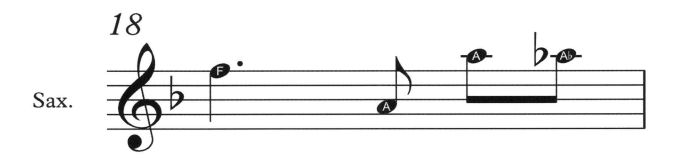
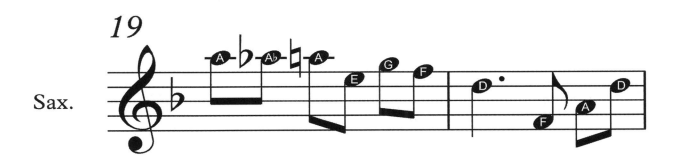

Eine Kleine Nachtmusik

Mozart

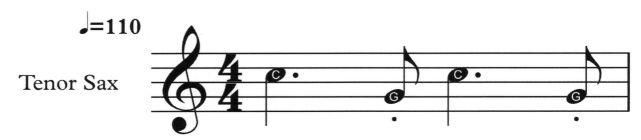

2

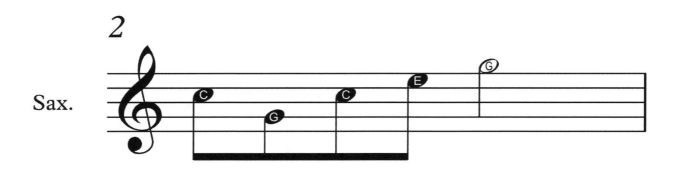

3

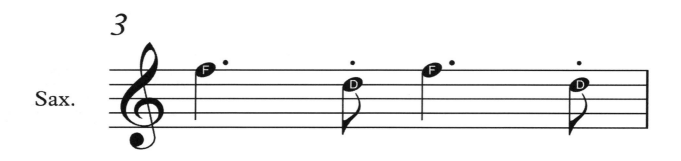

4

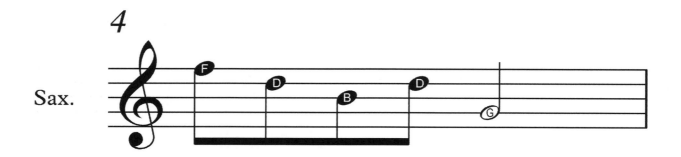

5

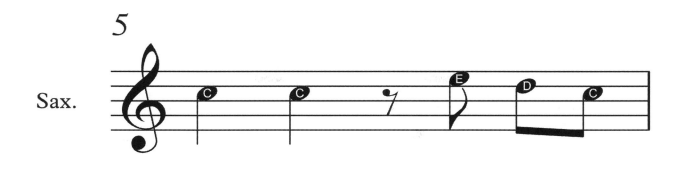

6

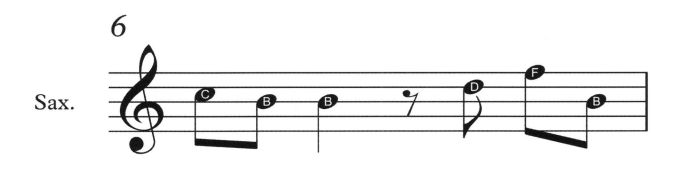

7

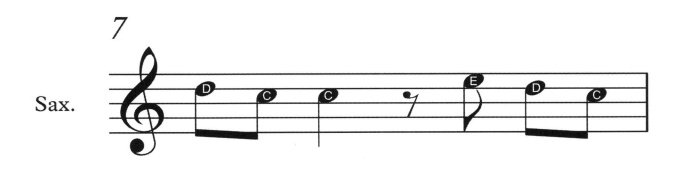

8

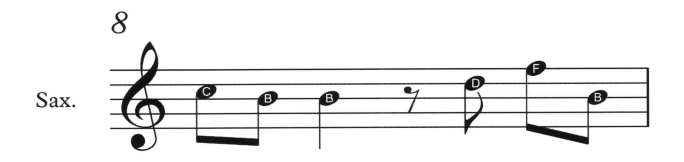

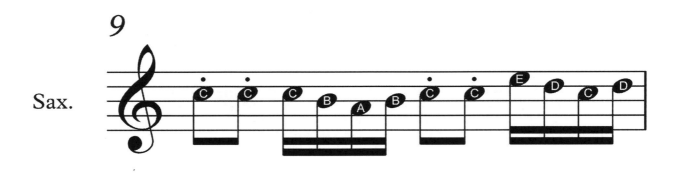

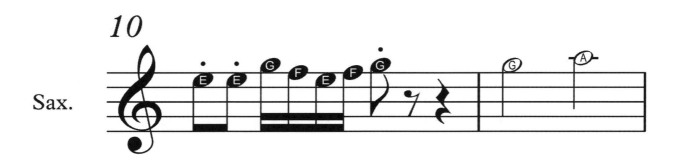

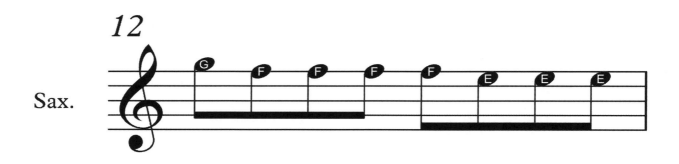

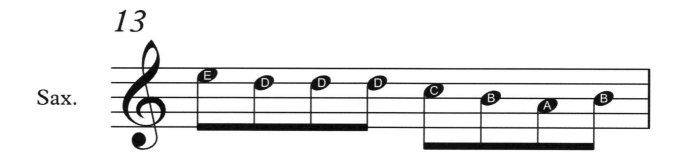

Home On The Range

Daniel E. Kelley

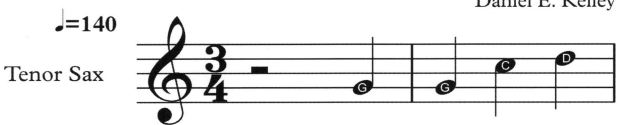
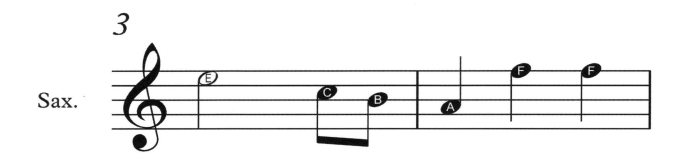
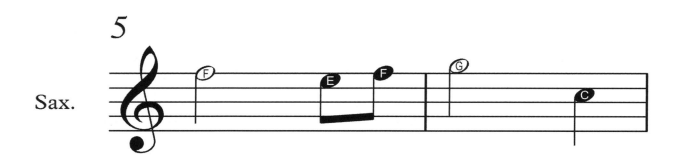
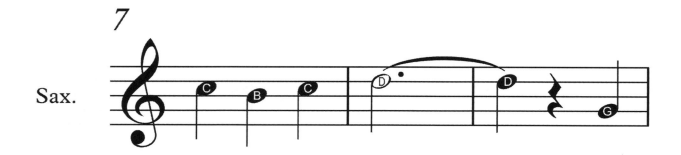

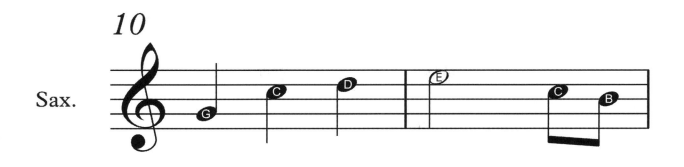
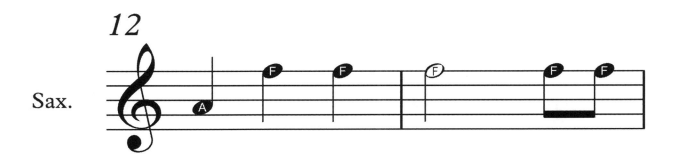

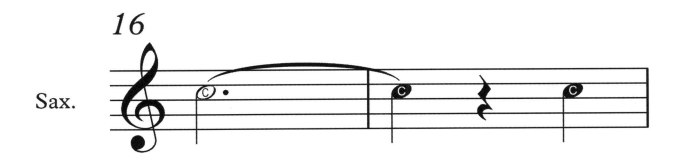

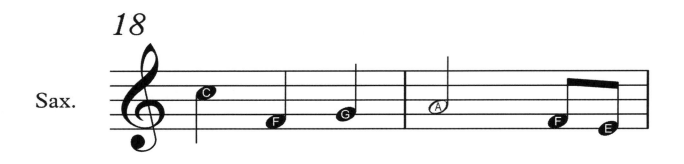
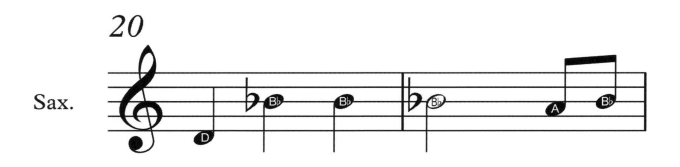
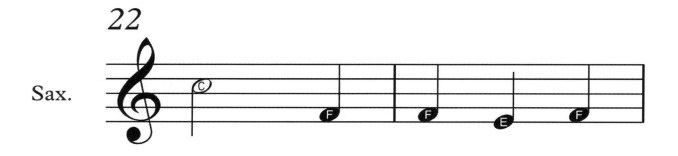
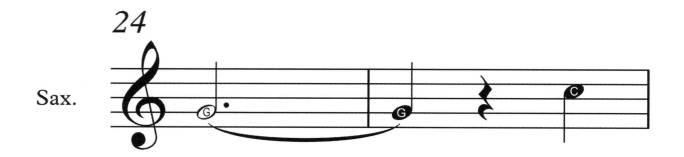

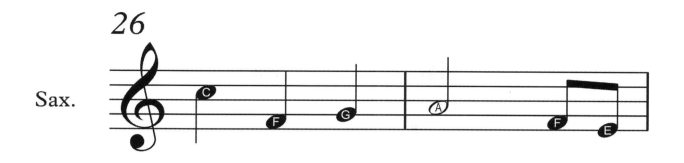
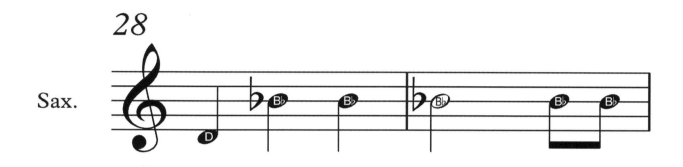
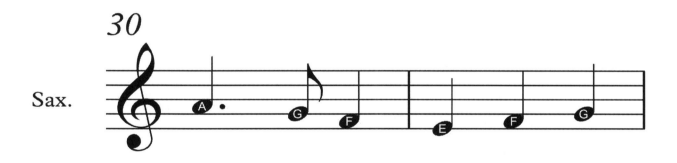
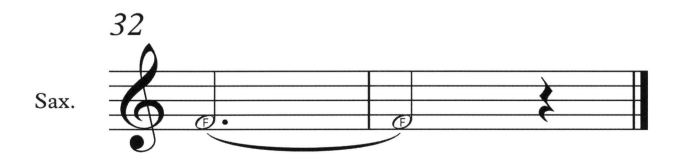

Liebestraum

Franz Liszt

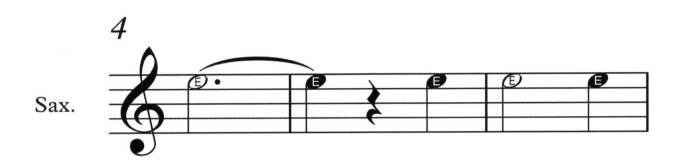

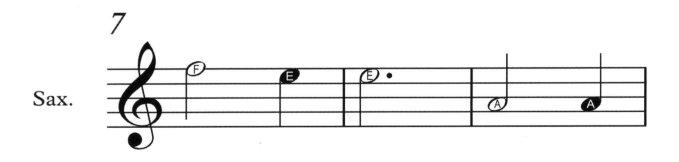

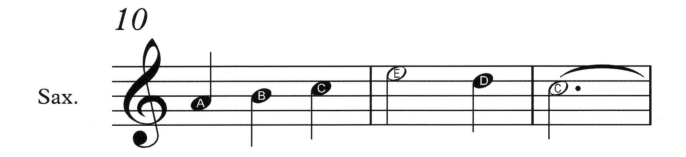

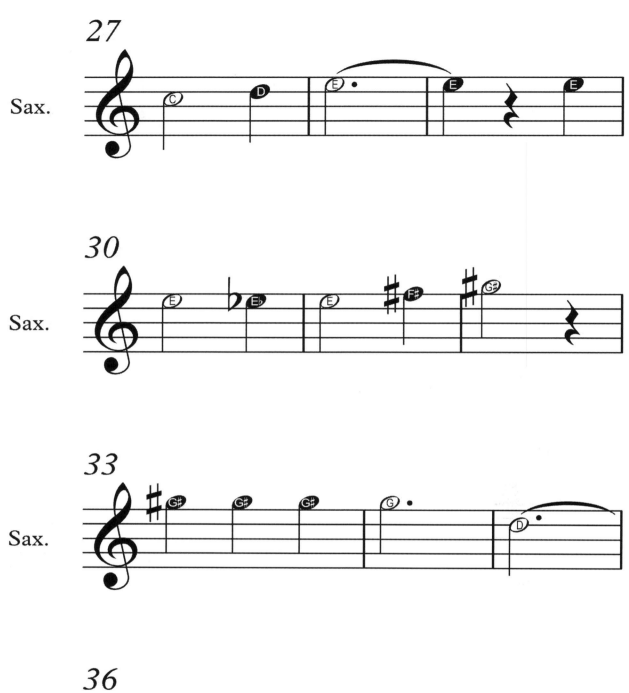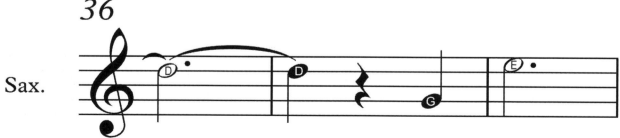

39

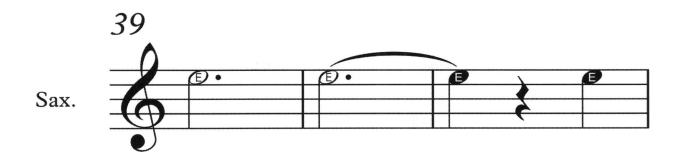

42

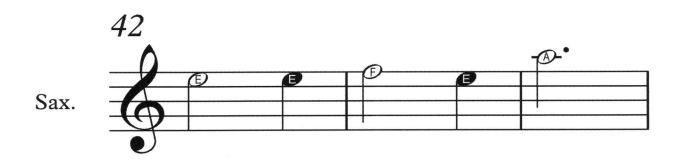

45

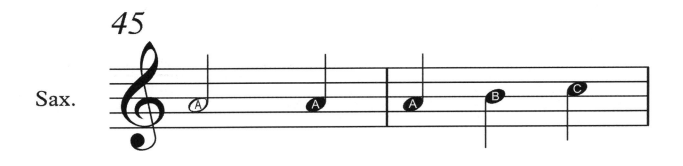

47

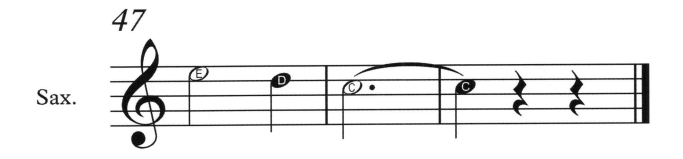

Lullabye

Brahms

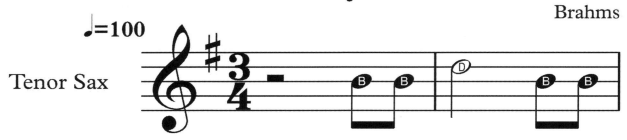
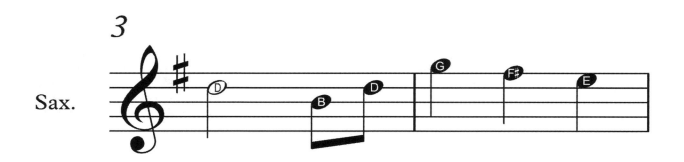
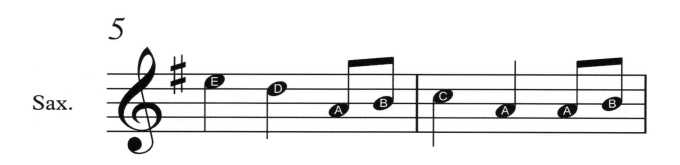
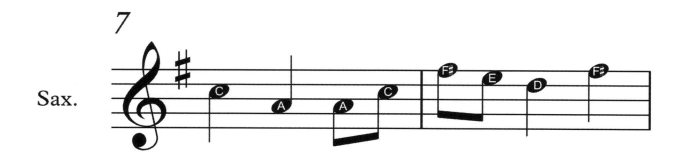

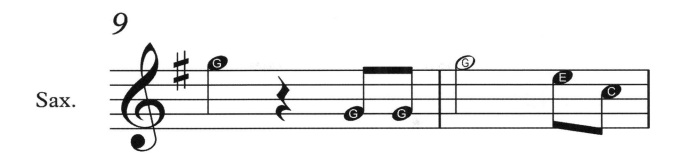
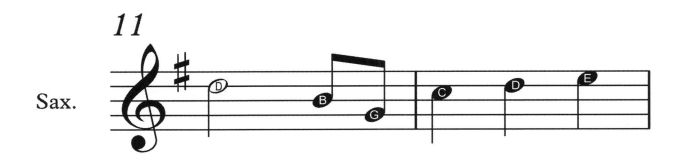
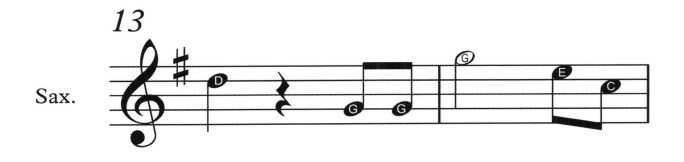
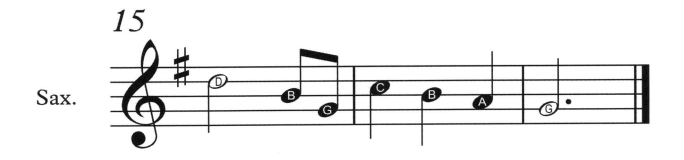

Michael Row The Boat Ashore

Traditional

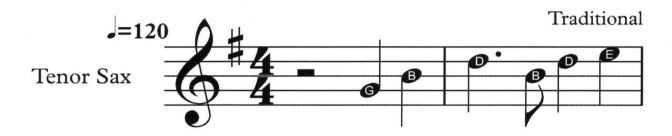

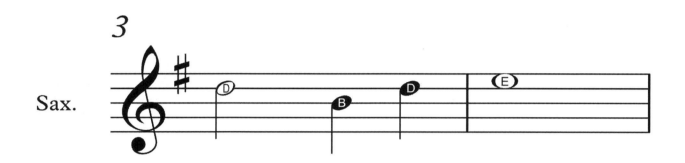

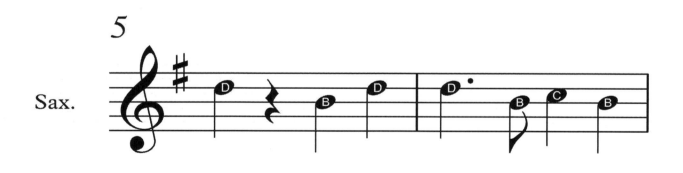

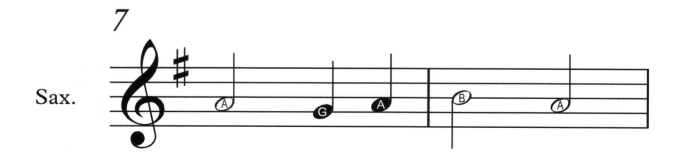

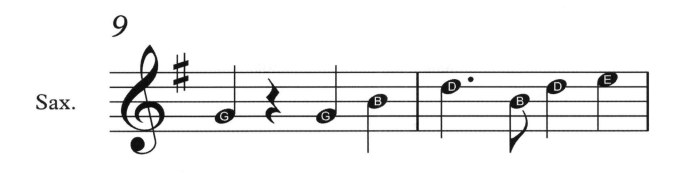
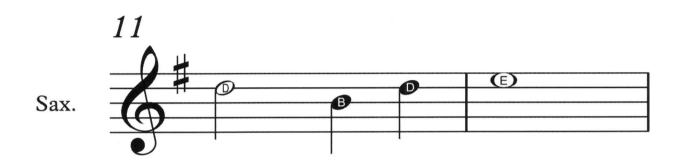
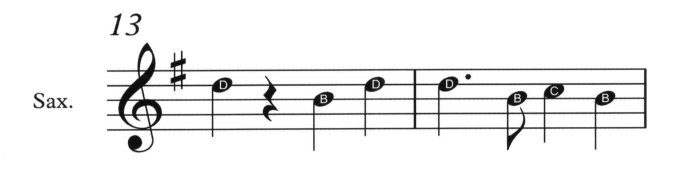
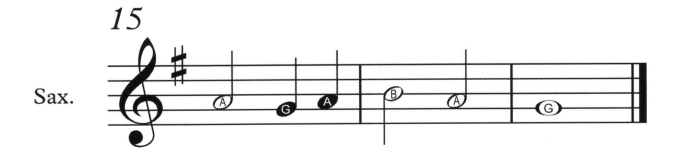

My Heart At Thy Sweet Voice

Camille Saint-Saëns

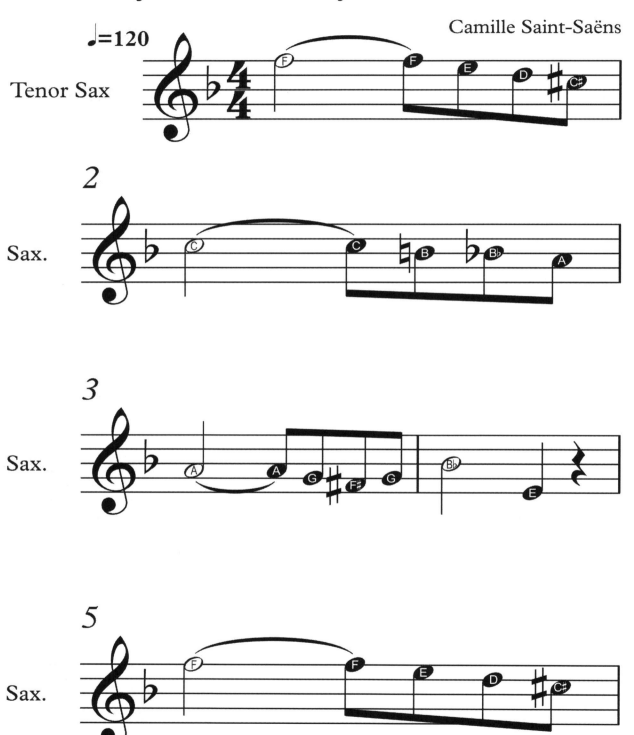

40

6

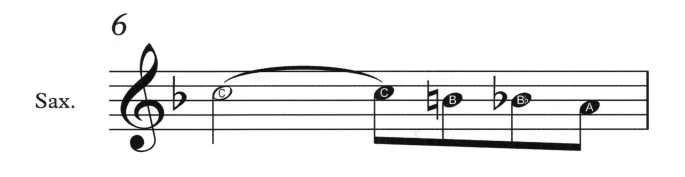

7

9

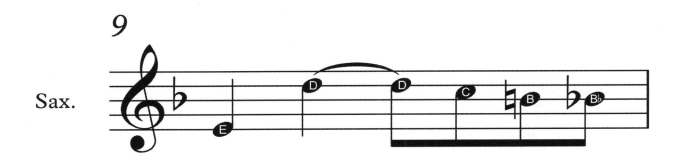

10

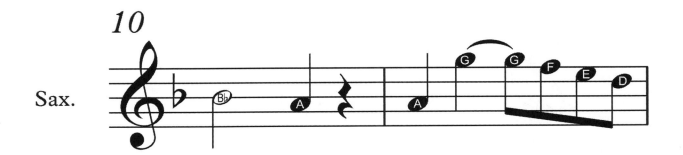

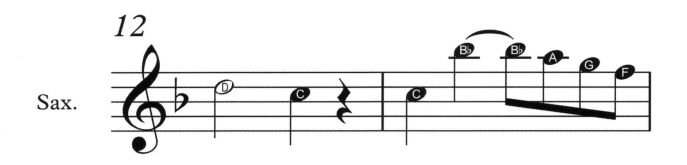
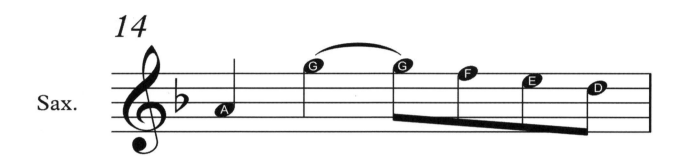
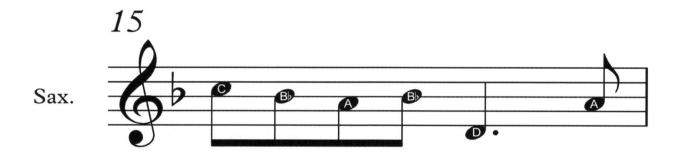
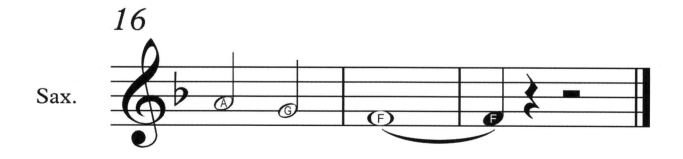

Oh Susanna

Traditional

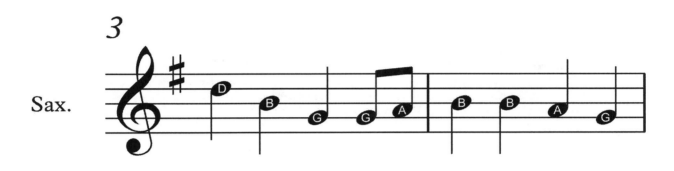
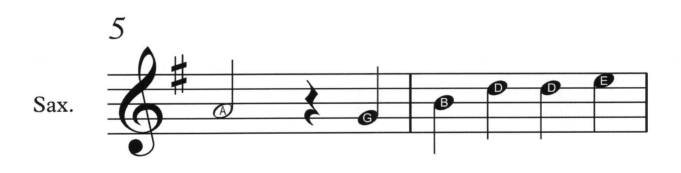
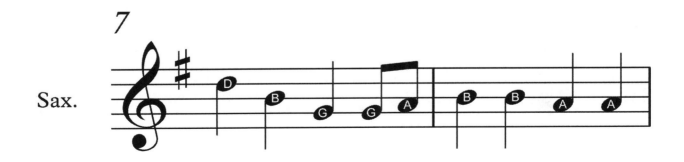

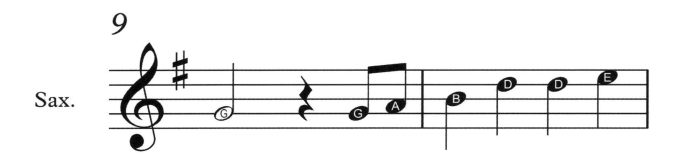
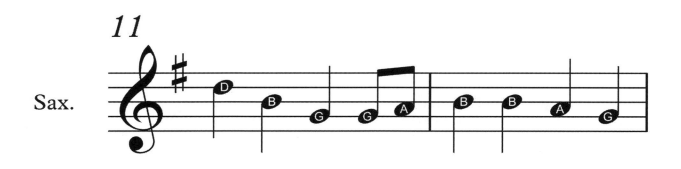
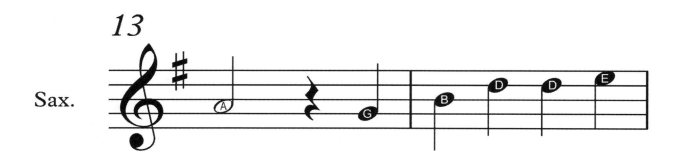
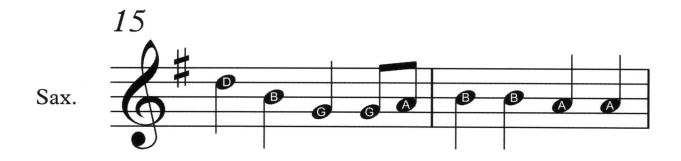

Piano Concerto No.1

Tchaikovsky

When The Saints Go Marching In

Tenor Sax — Traditional

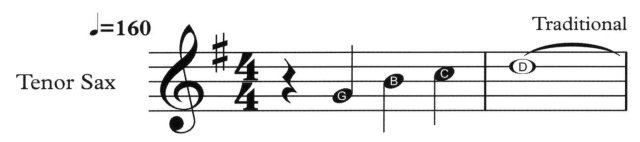

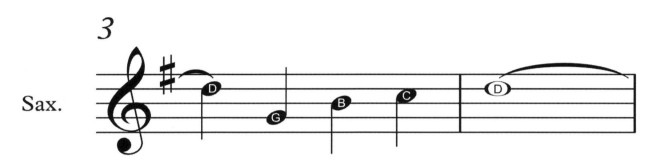

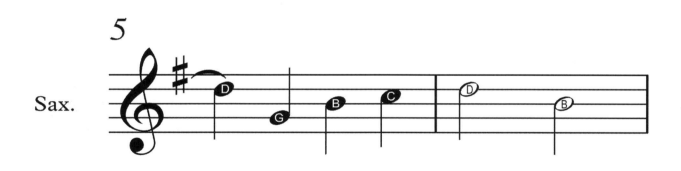

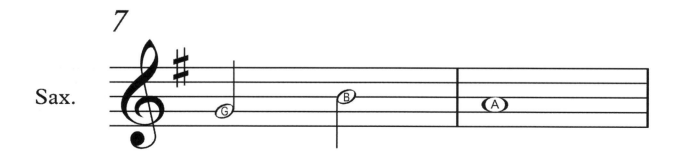

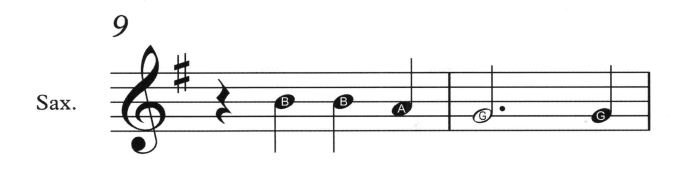
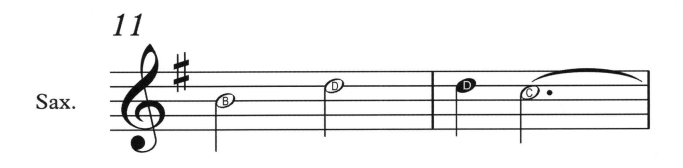
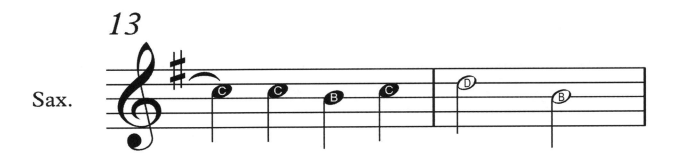
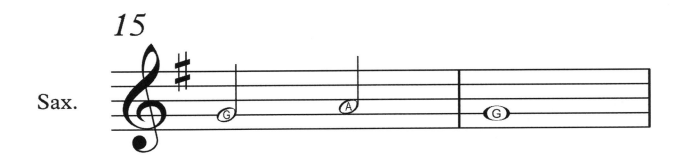

17

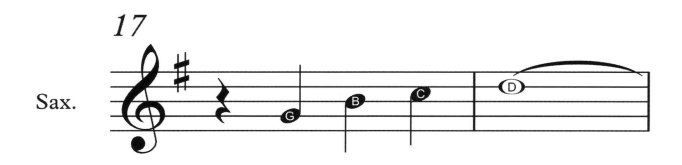

19

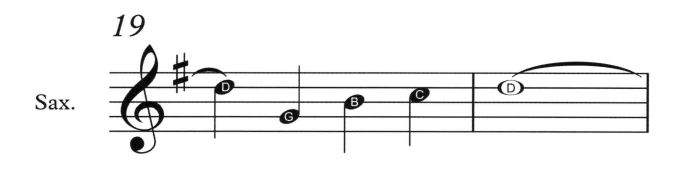

21

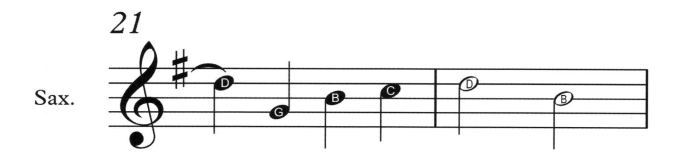

23

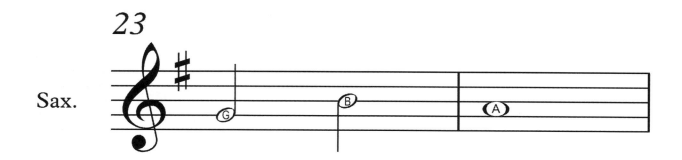

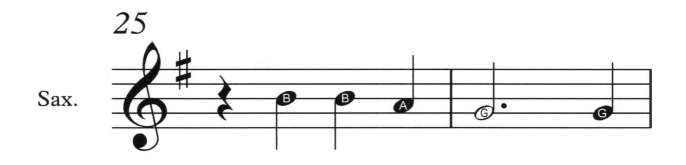
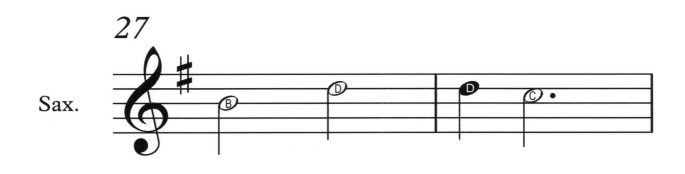
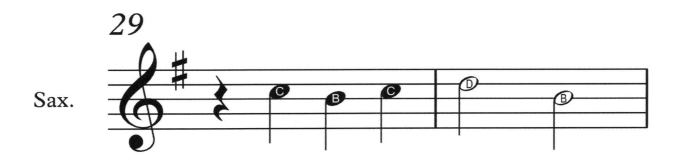
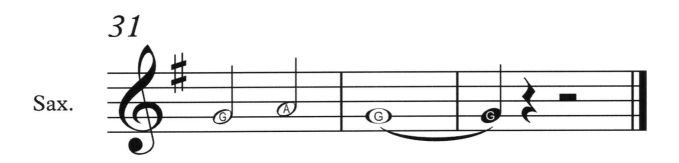

Sonata No.8 Pathetique

Beethoven

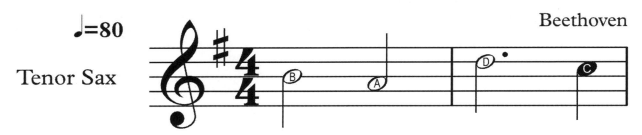
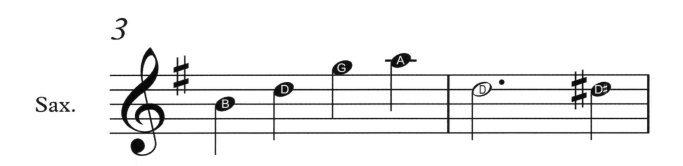
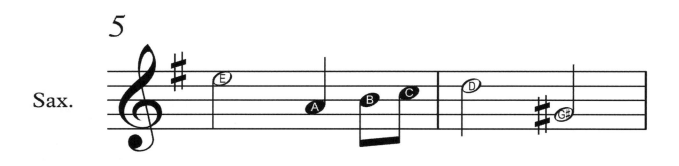
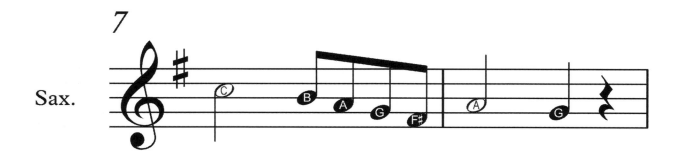

Valse Lente

Leo Delibes

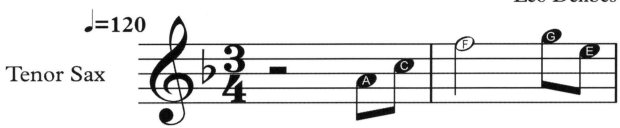
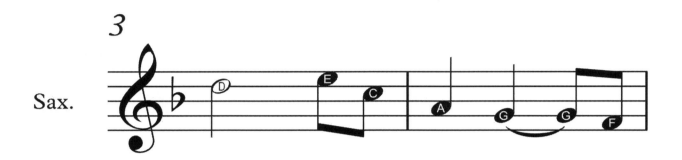
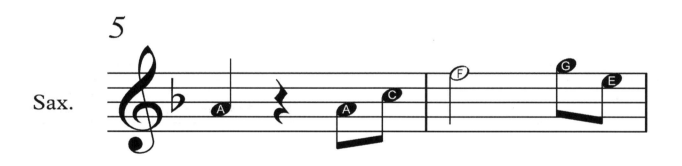
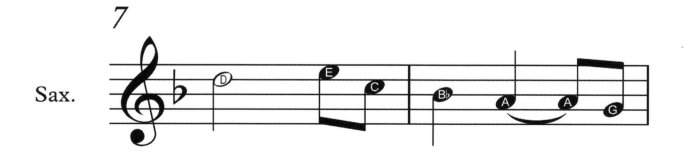

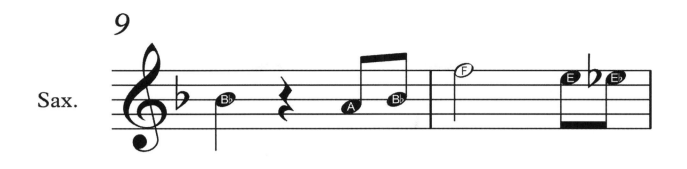
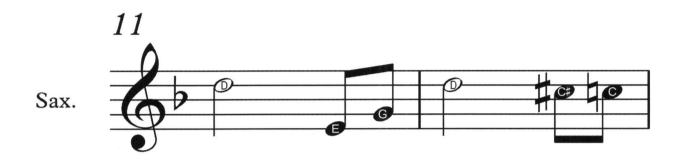
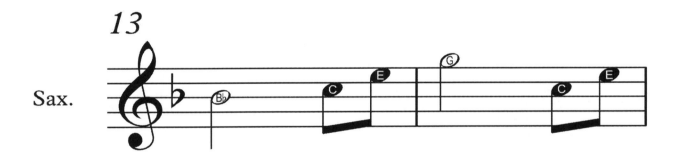
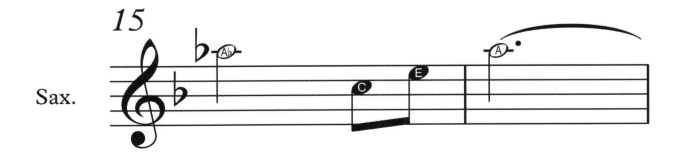

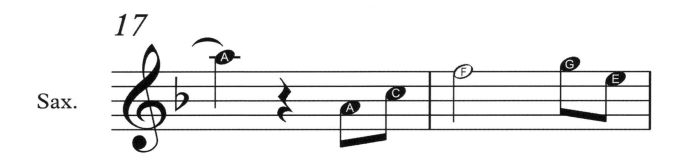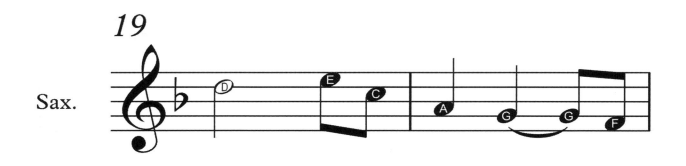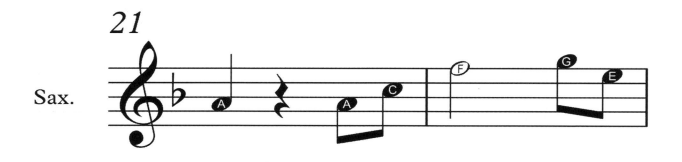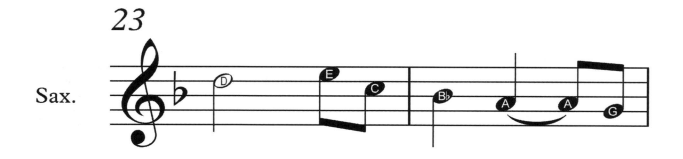

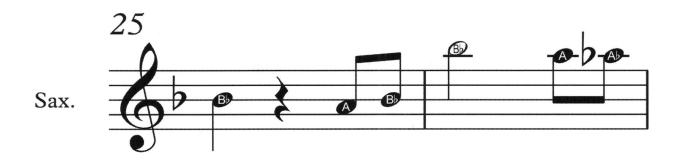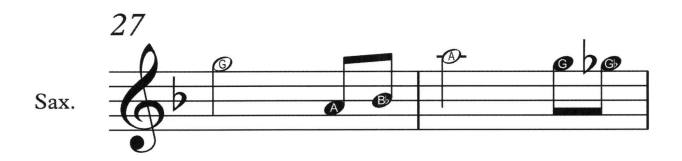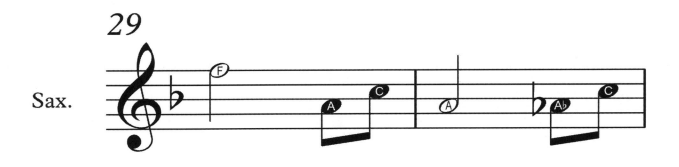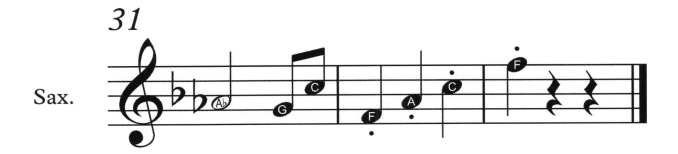

The Yellow Rose Of Texas

Traditional

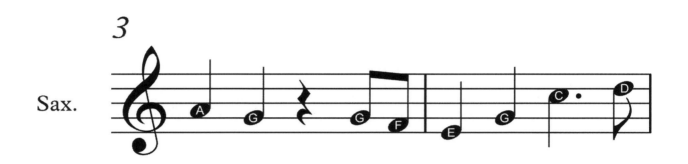

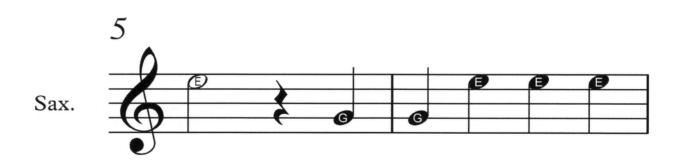

9

11

13

15

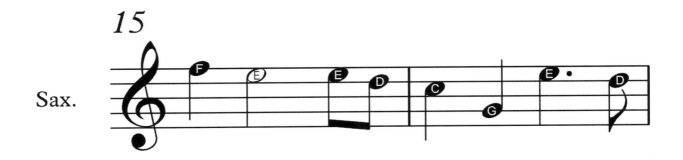

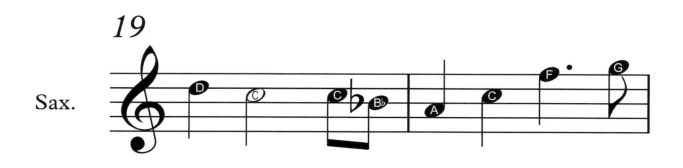

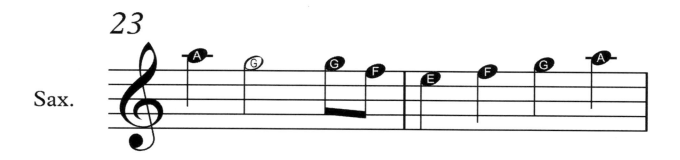

Trumpet Voluntary

Jeremiah Clarke

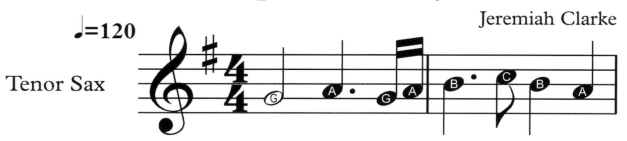
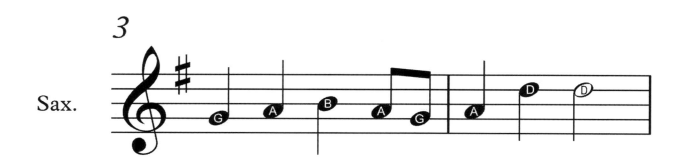
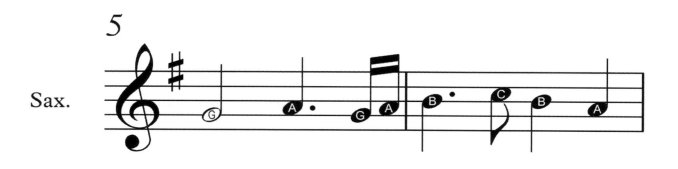
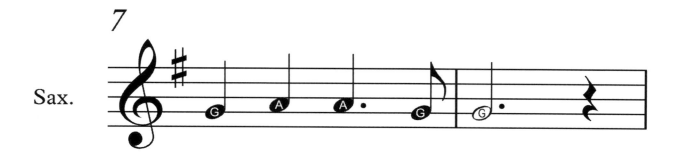

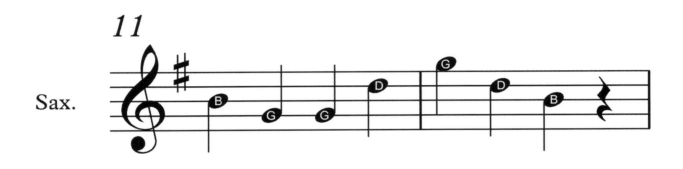

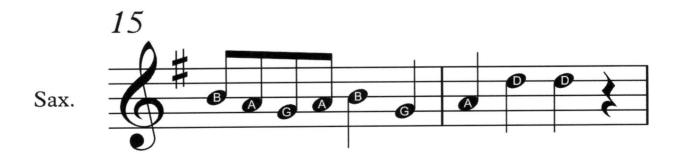

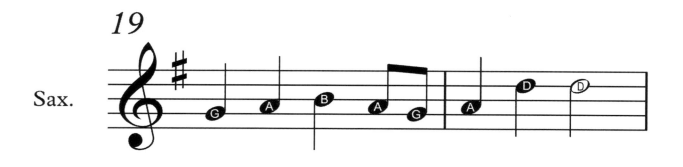
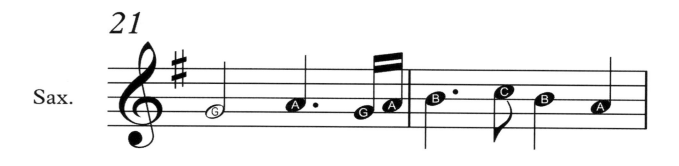

About the Author

Mike works as a professional musician and keyboard music teacher. Mike has been teaching piano, electronic keyboard and electric organ for over thirty years and as a keyboard player worked in many night clubs and entertainment venues.

Mike has also branched out in to composing music and has written and recorded many new royalty free tracks which are used worldwide in TV, film and internet media applications. Mike is also proud of the fact that many of his students have gone on to be musicians, composers and teachers in their own right.

You can connect with Mike at:

Facebook
facebook.com/keyboardsheetmusic

Soundcloud
soundcloud.com/audiomichaeld

YouTube
youtube.com/user/pianolessonsguru

I hope this book has helped you with your music, if you have received value from it in any way, then please leave a review and encourage like minded musical instrument players around the world to keep playing music.

Thank You
Michael Shaw

Manufactured by Amazon.ca
Bolton, ON